Swings and Roundabouts

Also by Glyn Goode:

No Beach left to Walk On: Poems of Reflection
2012. ISBN 978-1909304505

Pictures in the Sand: Poems of Contemplation
2013. ISBN 976-1909304154

Ebb and Flow: Poems of Reflection
2014. ISBN 978-1291911565

Available from Amazon and Kindle

Swings and Roundabouts

Poems of Contemplation

Glyn Goode

Swings and Roundabouts:
Poems of Contemplation

All Rights Reserved. Copyright © 2015 Glyn Goode

No part of this book may be reproduced or transmitted in any form or by any means, graphic, electronic, or mechanical, including photocopying, recording, taping or by any information storage or retrieval system, without the permission in writing from the copyright holder.

The right of Glyn Goode to be identified as the author of this work has been asserted in accordance with the Copyright, Designs and Patents Act 1988 sections 77 and 78.

The views expressed in this work are solely those of the author and do not necessarily reflect the views of the publisher, and the publisher hereby disclaims any responsibility for them.

ISBN: 978-1-909874-92-3

With thanks to

Charles H. Muller, MA, PhD
John E. Lucius
Joanne Moore

For their kind words and encouragement

TABLE OF CONTENTS

A BETTER LIFE	17	EASTER BUNNY	19
A LITTLE FLUTTER	4	EXCUSEZ MOI	16
A LOVING SEED	8	FLOWER OF ENGLAND	31
A NOTE TO MYSELF	39	FRUITY	26
A SCOTTISH GENTLEMAN	33	FUNFAIR OF LOVE	40
		GENIUS	52
A STATE OF MIND	48	GHOST TRAIN	48
ADIEU	5	HANDLE WITH CARE	11
AIR MAIL	51	HOPEFUL	37
AND THEY'RE OFF	51	ICE AGE	50
AND YOU ARE	24	ICON	35
ANIMAL CRACKERS	47	IN WITH THE NEW	1
APRIL SHOWER	27	JOY	44
ASPIRATION	41	JUST DANDY	5
AT FACE VALUE	50	JUST LAZY	53
BANK HOLIDAY	52	JUST LUCK	45
BEHIND THE MASK	32	KARA	19
BLESSED	12	LEFTOVERS	16
BLIND FAITH	22	LIE IN	31
BLOB	49	ME MYSELF AND NOBODY ELSE	18
CAUGHT SHORT	38		
CHRISTMAS	11	MIRAGE	42
CLEANSED	34	MYSTICAL	23
CRASH LANDING	53	NAIL THE SUCKER	20
DASTARDLY DEED	36	NEW DAY	12
DAY TRIPPER	28	NICE TO BE NICE	20
DON'T BE CONNED	27	NIGHTMARE	7

NIGHTSHIFT	9
NO I DON'T KNOW	36
NO STORY	49
NOT TONIGHT LOVE	45
NOW WE ARE ONE	46
NUTTY	23
OLD HAT	21
ONE LAST WALK	7
ONLY A GAME	28
ONLY ME	46
OOPS	26
PARTICIPATE	6
PESTS	44
PLAYTHING	30
READY MEAL	51
REASON TO BE JOYFUL	10
REMORSELESS	37
SEASONS	32
SHUSH	25
SIMPLE THINGS	38
SLIPPERY TOAD AHEAD	14
SLY OLD FOX	33
SPINNING	43
STUNG	13
SWIMMING LESSON	53
SWINGS AND ROUNDABOUTS	29
THE GRASS ISN'T ALWAYS GREENER	2
THE KEEPER	13
THE WISHING WELL IS DRY	43
TONGUE TIED	41
TRANQUIL	3
UMBRELLA	18
UNBLINKERED	10
UNCORK	3
VAMPIRES	46
WEATHER FORECAST	4
WORLDS APART	42
WRONG DIRECTIONS	45

IN WITH THE NEW

To young people I say
Don't be swayed by thoughts of yesterday
For you are greatly maligned
By people whose eyes are blind
If you have an idea be brave
Perhaps the world you could save
Don't be dictated by convention
You are the mother of your own invention.

Young ideas will be refreshing
Compared to the old window dressing
With your new ideas the world can change
Not old policies just rearranged
Sweet young thoughts are nice
Not tainted by your elders vice.

One day you will leave your teens
But never let go of your dreams
I'm glad you young people are here
You fill an old mans heart with cheer
Because you have so much to give
Please grab your life and live.

THE GRASS ISN'T ALWAYS GREENER

It's just a nondescript lane
Leading to a cottage that's almost mundane
Customary roses over the front door
With a stone kitchen floor.

Mother with her apron around the waist
Cooking tasteful treats for us to taste
Dad in the garden, vegetables growing
Love all around us, overflowing.

Simple things like a loving kiss
Toasting muffins over the log fire, bliss
Now I have my own family
Kids playing around the apple tree
Friends ask, why do you stay
Simple, we're happy here every day.

TRANQUIL

Flowers with early morning dew
Images of you come into view
You have a beauty so refined
An unadulterated mind
With you peace I can find
Smell the flowers, take my time
For you are the placid sea
That brought me tranquillity.

UNCORK

We are waiting to hear
The thoughts you hold dear
Don't lock them away
Give them the light of day
Your mind may be reeling
Speak out, express your feeling
Put those thoughts on paper
Now, today, not later
Don't be silent, be heard
Use the written word
Don't think you are alone
For you are not on your own.

A LITTLE FLUTTER

Told my friend I'm backing this horse
It's good for the course
I don't gamble said my friend
It's just a means to an end
Life is just a gamble I said
Every day when you get out of bed.

WEATHER FORECAST

Clouds cover the sunshine
Blur the hurt in my mind
Events turning my heart
Tearing my body apart.
Once my life was bliss
Now no one my tears to kiss
It's starting to rain
Is this love's last refrain
To you I am speaking
But you are not listening.

ADIEU

All your pain I feel
It makes my mind reel
Your skin you try to peel
The trauma to reveal
It tortures your mind
For no relief can you find.
My tears start to swell
Because your life is hell
Your last wish I'll honour my friend
The agony will now come to an end.

JUST DANDY

I've sown many a wayward seed
People think I'm just a weed
I'm an unwanted flower
But I have a lot of power
And I can be relied upon
For I am a dandelion
Look out your window at dawn
I'll be all over your lawn.

PARTICIPATE

Golfers have a round
Boxers fight pound for pound
You're leg before wicket
When playing cricket
Rugby has a funny shaped ball
Sport really is for all
Athletics will get you fit
Make sure you have the kit
Taking part in sport can be fun
Just go along and have a run.

NIGHTMARE

Dark thoughts cradle you to sleep
Back of your mind to keep
Demons are spitting fire
In you fear they inspire
Moon sitting high in the sky
Phantoms floating by.

In a cold sweat you awake
It's almost daybreak
Tears fall from the eye
You release a welcome sigh
A new day is starting
The nightmare is departing.

ONE LAST WALK

Here comes the hangman with his noose
Another soul to let loose
You start to shed a tear
While trying to hide your fear
But if you take someones life
Expect to pay the ultimate price.

A LOVING SEED

This ogre was living in a cave
A monster who would rant and rave
Trees with his bare hands he would uproot
Just because he could, for a hoot
With his bouts of mindless violence
The peasants would fall into silence
They would run a mile
If they saw him smile
In his frustration he would stomp the ground
Tremors were felt for miles around.

One day a young lad broke his leg
Help me mister ogre please did he beg
He picked him up with one arm
And took him to the nearest farm
So by his caring deed
He sowed a loving seed.

For he only wanted to be their friend
His loneliness to end
The pain in his eyes they couldn't see
For he was the only ogre in the territory
Now in their gratitude
The people leave the kind ogre food.

NIGHTSHIFT

Long into lonely night
I sit at my table and write
Music playing away
At the end of a weary day
Taking a few beers
And shedding some tears
I write into early morn
When new lines are born
After a while I sleep
New lines in my mind to keep.

When the morning dawns and I'm sober
Those lines I'll check over
Some I may use again
In a different refrain.

UNBLINKERED

There is nothing you cannot achieve
If in yourself you believe
If in your mind there is doubt
Open your eyes and look out.

REASON TO BE JOYFUL

I was very low, quite down
My face was one big frown
But at last I've something to cheer
Celebrate and have a beer
This day I never thought I would see
My Stephanie holding her own baby.
Such a fragile bundle of joy
A beautiful baby boy
Now I am no longer sad
For she has made me a granddad.

HANDLE WITH CARE

Today is a new dawn
For a baby has been born
Sent to us by God above
Welcomed into our family with love
Your life has just begun
Say hello to the world, Logan.

CHRISTMAS

A day that should be profound
Is driven by the pound
Get people to spend at will
As long as they fill our till
A time that should be nice
Is filled with total avarice.

BLESSED

I know a girl with a really beautiful mind
Better it would be hard to find
She wasn't born in a manger
But peaceful without any anger
Beauty and wisdom beyond her years
Her compassion brings me to tears
To life she gives music and laughter
I'm so blessed because she's my daughter.

NEW DAY

Oh the joy of early dawn
As a new day is born
Pale light low in the sky
Songbirds singing on high
The light now is brighter
As the sun rises higher
Throw that duvet away
Arise and greet this new day.

STUNG

Once I took her out
This little mange tout
But she dumped me
For this little bee.

THE KEEPER

To the chapel I took a walk
See the main man, have a talk
Things I need to ask him about
Because I have this doubt
Troubling things in my mind
I can no longer hide
So I looked the big man in the eye
To him you do not lie
In my eyes he sees tears
He knows all my fears
Things I cannot hide
Because he can reach deep inside
He allowed my life to evolve
For he is the keeper of my soul.

SLIPPERY TOAD AHEAD

Strolling along a country road
I found my way hindered
By an enormous toad
Thinking he was hurt
And I being a caring soul
I stopped and offered him help
Are you alright I ask.
Oh yes thank you, he croaks
By the way before you pass
Have you paid your road tax
But dear sir I do say
I have no car
So I have not rode
So I have no tax to pay
But here's a kiss and a cuddle
And I will be on my way.

After a while I met Mrs Hare
Good day Mrs Hare I do say
Isn't this a lovely day
Yes it is, she says
Did you meet Mr Toad on your way
Yes I did, I reply.
Did you pay his tax
Oh no, I gave him a kiss
And went on my way.
That was for the best
Don't bother about him
He's just trying to feather his own nest.

Come Mrs Hare, let's have a cup of tea.
Now that would be nice
There's a cafe just around the bend
It's owned by my friend
Her name is Mrs Mole
And it's called 'Toad in the hole.'
After we had had our tea
I thanked Mrs Hare and Mrs Mole.
Mrs Hare said, have you further to roam
No I am nearly there, said I
As I wished them both goodbye
And went on my way home.

As I approached home
I saw this figure standing alone
Oh no, not you again Mr Toad.
Yes sorry he says
But again I have to ask
Can you please give to my tax
For I am trying to raise enough money
So I can build a tunnel
So all of us toads
Can safely cross the road.

Now he can sit back and relax
For he'd collected enough tax
Work on his tunnel can now begin
No wonder he has a big grin.
He was treated like a fool
Now he sits high on his stool.

LEFTOVERS

Loves light now long gone
In the murky mist, undone
A stone trodden in the ground
Out of sight never to be found
Clouds of swirling grey
Lost in a never ending day
Darkness lifts from the sky
Rain washes away the sigh
Love now long dead
Images linger in the head.

EXCUSEZ MOI

After a night of lager and curry
I usually end up in a hurry
So if you will pardon me
There's a certain place I need to be.

A BETTER LIFE

I knew that one day
Fame and fortune would come my way
I'd be recognised walking down the street
Famous people I would meet.

It came with a slap in the face
Just shallow people all over the place
How I now long for the old me
And the way things used to be.

Those long ago early years
Although there was worry and tears
People you knew and could trust
Without the never-ending monetary lust.

Go to a football game and cheer
And afterwards have a beer
I may not be poor now
But that world seemed better somehow.

ME MYSELF AND NOBODY ELSE

There are times I need to be alone
By myself in my own zone
Enjoy the peace and quiet of mind
My inner self to find
No newspaper telling me what to think
So called experts saying what to eat or drink.

Just sit on a deserted beach
No one else in reach
Feel the breeze thro' my hair
A few moments without a care
Sitting there by myself
Alone with no one else.

UMBRELLA

You are the light
In my dark night
Your smile eased my pain
Sunshine after the rain
You gave me hope
Without you I couldn't cope.

KARA

You are a sweet beautiful girl Kara
Your young life has been full of trauma
At a young age you died
But thankfully you were revived
You were sent to us by angels above
And now you have found love
I hope your future years
Will bring you no more tears.

EASTER BUNNY

I'm not loved by farmers
And detested by gardeners
But I've told you before
On carrots I like to gnaw
I know I go on a bit
But I'm only a little rabbit.

NICE TO BE NICE

Perhaps your mind I may entice
It's beautiful to be nice
So don't be rash and hasty
For it's ugly to be nasty.

NAIL THE SUCKER

In the early hours I was awoken
To the police station I was taken
Just to help with their questioning
As an experience it was arresting
Got away with it so I thought
But I still got caught
The hanging judge I have to meet
Because accidently I dropped paper in the street.

OLD HAT

Glastonbury yawn, what a bore
Old bands by the score
How long can it last
For it's living in the past
In its infancy it was grand
Gave young bands a helping hand
Now it's 'I say by golly'
Let's go to Glastonbury for a jolly
Turn up in their luxury campervan
Look at me, I'm the main man.

For new singers it was their first big gig
Now a gathering of pompous prigs
The Stones and Parton have made their money
Let the young taste the honey.

BLIND FAITH

It's a cross that we bear
For our allegiance we did swear
A red cross on white cloth
On our chest we do doth
We turn out game after game
Are we completely insane
But England is our country
So we just do our duty.

Football is not just a bug
It's our never-ending drug
We hope for fame and glory
But that's just a fairy story
Never mind, we still go to the game
Although the results are the same.

MYSTICAL

I'm half asleep, not fully awake
It's nowhere near daybreak
Suddenly on comes the bedside light
Now I'm fully awake, with a fright
I didn't switch it on
Could it be an astral phenomenon
Or a dear departed one from high above
Sending me their love.

NUTTY

I'm a squirrel, I live in trees
Easy going, not hard to please
I'm up the tree and down
Scavenge on the ground
Life is full of 'ifs' and 'buts'
I cannot remember where I buried my nuts.

AND YOU ARE

Do you really exist
Are you the swirling mist
A ray of sunlight
The moons soft glow at night
Dark clouds on high
Rain from the sky
A bee buzzing by
The spider catching a fly
Young bird fresh on the wing
Just starting to sing
The early morning dew
Just who are you.

SHUSH

At noon he rode into town
On his face a frown
The stranger sat for a while
Tight lipped, no smile
When he strode the sidewalk
There was no idle talk
A time to back down
Because the stranger was in town.

A lone figure stood in the street
This is the man he came to meet
A single shot was the only sound
As the man fell to the ground
Upright and tall the stranger rode away
Not a word did he speak that day.

OOPS

Crossing the ocean by sail
When I saw this whale
He didn't seem to have a care
Only came up for air
Thought my boat was a mate
Came charging in and bang, too late
Told him you're for the high jump
But he just snorted and took the hump.

FRUITY

I came into this world in a rush
Born under a gooseberry bush
I can be quite prickly
Is that why I'm so finicky.

APRIL SHOWER

The touch of your body still lingers
On the tips of my fingers
The smell of you is still in the air
As is the colour of your hair
So please at this late hour
Could you just take a shower.

DON'T BE CONNED

There are people sowing the seeds
For you to commit evil deeds
Saying what is wrong and right
Craven cowards telling you to fight
Telling you that everything in heaven is fine
It's not their lives on the line.

Life is not as they want you to see
It's what you can make it be
If you have a loving soul
A better life can evolve
If you don't believe religious doctrine
A better life for you can begin.

DAY TRIPPER

It flew by so fast
At a speed I couldn't grasp
In the sky a glowing light
But it wasn't a satellite
What it was I really don't know
My friends said it was a 'UFO'

Earth is an extremely savage place
So why would we get tourists from outer space.

ONLY A GAME

Sitting on the stair
Hands in my hair
Tears run down my cheek
Distraught, cannot speak
Things will never be the same
But wait, football is only a game
Relegated but there was a reason
And next year is another season.

SWINGS AND ROUNDABOUTS

Remember as a kid going to the fair
On the rides, wind blowing thro' your hair
Toffee apples and popcorn
Can we stay till dawn
All the noise and commotion
A magical potion
The waltzers and big wheel
Nothing seemed real
It was all so wild
The joys of being a child.

PLAYTHING

Although you're by my side
Something is dying inside
You are speaking to me
But my pain you cannot see
Can't you feel my heart
It's breaking apart.

My mind is in a whirl
So happy because you're my girl
Love, oh sweet love
Thought you were sent from heaven above
Enclosed by a consuming joy
But I am just your toy.

FLOWER OF ENGLAND

A sweet flower of delight
Shining in summers light
It does not need to pose
The beautiful English rose.

Its petals you can use
Just let them fuse
They will make a lovely scent
That's almost heaven-sent
Rosehips make a delicate wine
Sweet as the grape from the vine.

LIE IN

Have you ever had a day
When nothing goes your way
Get up in the morning feeling strong
Then everything goes wrong
Does it make you feel
That this world is not real
If you knew it would be this way
You'd have stopped in bed all day.

SEASONS

All the flowers in the spring
Cannot make my heart sing
Swallows soaring in a summer sky
Cannot end this endless sigh
Autumn leaves fallen from trees
Blown by an emotionless breeze
Winter nights now so cold
Frozen by the lies you told.

BEHIND THE MASK

Does anyone know what it's like to fall
Continuously into a brick wall
Forever walking up an endless hill
Ground down by an emotionless mill
Head resting on the window pane
Smeared by tears as if by rain
When day is blacker than night
With no end to your emotional plight.

SLY OLD FOX

There was this man from Wainfleet
Not the sort you would like to meet
Seems as if he doesn't make a fuss
But he's a cunning old cuss
Buy me a pint and I'll get the next one
But when you've supped up, he's long gone.

A SCOTTISH GENTLEMAN

There is a person I know named Eugene
Nicest man I've ever seen
Born in the land of the Scots
Which he has never forgot
A man of unassuming charm
Who will do nobody any harm
Ever ready with a joke
An out and out decent bloke
Always a smile on his face
A credit to the human race.

CLEANSED

You appeared through a swirling mist
My doubts you cast adrift
A smile that washed away my tears
With laughter that eased the fears
When my life was full of sorrow
You gave me a tomorrow
Your love engulfs me
The horizon I can now see.

ICON

With his flowing locks of golden hair
He drove that McLaren without a care
Drove flat out, hell-for-leather
Who cares about the weather
Trash the tyres to the rim
Determination coursing from within.

A young flamboyant playboy
To watch him on the track was a joy
Ever relentless for the win
And always that endearing grin
The Grand Prix was his fix
His passion was to race, socialise and mix.

He was a Great English icon
One of the few, alas now gone
Affectionately known as 'The Shunt'
Gone but not forgotten, the enigmatic James Hunt.

NO I DON'T KNOW

My anger I have to show
For people who keep saying 'You know'
If the answer I knew
I would not have asked you
Is it such a hard task
To answer the question I ask.

I know where this came from
From the people who only know how to bomb
I am not being vague
'You know' is spreading like a plague
And I'm not being pedantic
But it came from across the Atlantic.

DASTARDLY DEED

When I was young and impressionable
I committed a crime that was terrible
A deed I cannot now take back
I bought a record by Cilla Black.

REMORSELESS

An endless spiralling staircase
Things said in haste
Good deeds cast aside
Buried, trying to hide
No more sky of blue
Nothing left to do
A dark room without light
No more vision or sight.

HOPEFUL

Seeing children with smiles on their face
Take me to a magical place
A beautiful wonderland
Where happy dreams abound
A place for them to enjoy
Every girl and boy
Play all day and night
Be happy without fear or fright.

SIMPLE THINGS

I don't ask much
Just a hug, a loving touch
A simple kiss
Little things I really miss
But these things are denied me
For reasons I cannot see.

CAUGHT SHORT

I am just a little cat
And I sleep on a mat
On your garden I leave my stool
What's wrong with that you fool
That's why I am alive
For gardens to fertilise
Hey wait, put that shotgun down
There are other gardens around.

A NOTE TO MYSELF

A memo to my mind
Who is it inside
What thoughts do I hide
Are there things I need to confide
Questions constantly arise
No answers, that's not a surprise
Thoughts are like a birds wing
A very fragile thing.

FUNFAIR OF LOVE

Love and pride
It's an eerie ride
A helter-skelter
Warm shelter
Smiles and frowns
Ups and downs
Many tears cried
A carousel ride
Scary ghost train
Sunshine and rain
Waltzers spinning you around
Dizzy on uneven ground.

Love is a big wheel
Makes your mind reel
A coconut shy
Makes you wonder why.

ASPIRATION

It's nice to have a dream
A plan, a scheme
I'm so happy for you
Because your dream has come true.

TONGUE TIED

A story of love never told
Pages never evolved
Words left unsaid
Unspoken in my head
Emotions held back
Never let off the track
Not allowed to talk
Could not do the walk
Things never tried
Tongue tied.

MIRAGE

On holiday relaxing, floating on the sea
When a mermaid swam alongside me
I thought this was a fantasy
These creatures cannot be
But there she was with beauty beyond compare
A loving smile and long flowing hair
Sun shimmers on the waves
A beautiful image to save.

WORLDS APART

I knew this girl from Scunthorpe
She could read my every thought
Told me my mind is in a mess
She knew I was from Skegness
For it's in a parallel universe
Where things are in reverse
In her world people work then play
Here they just booze all day.

THE WISHING WELL IS DRY

Today I glimpsed the sky
Black clouds are gathering on high
A bad day is looming from the east
The cloven one has been unleashed
Soon all things will be undone
No longer a warm morning sun
Too late to visit the wishing well
The gates have been opened to hell.

SPINNING

My senses were numb
But now they're undone
What was the chance
That a passing glance
Would send my mind in a whirl
You are a special girl.

JOY

Summers soft gentle breeze
Caressing the flowers and trees
Sea and sand under bare feet
A special treat
Bees leaving their hive
It's good to be alive.

PESTS

We are only mice
And life is not nice
Tortured and preyed upon
What wrong have we done
In the church we are quiet
And we control our diet
So please give us a rest
It's you humans who are the pest.

NOT TONIGHT LOVE

I knew a girl who was hard to bed
Always said she had an aching head
So I carried a packet of aspirin
Before her headaches could begin.

JUST LUCK

I've done many things in my life
But I've never taken a wife
When asked why I never had a bride
I replied luck was on my side.

WRONG DIRECTIONS

I thought my Sat.Nav was playing tricks
It sent me across a river called Styx
Now this isn't a place I should be
There are things a sane being should not see
It's the realm of the satanic sick
Run by a thing with legs like sticks
Think it's time to reverse my track
And send this Sat.Nav back.

ONLY ME

I am what I am
A solitary man
I go my own way
From day to day
For when all is said and done
I can rely on no one.

VAMPIRES

Nurses are really not nice, for example
I was asked to give a blood sample
For compassion they really do lack
They never give your blood back.

NOW WE ARE ONE

First time ever we made love
The heavens opened above
Stars exploded in the skies
Your soft sweet sighs
Our souls merging into one
Emotions at last in unison.

ANIMAL CRACKERS

I saw a panther coloured pink
Wow, that really made me think.

Jerry was a pesky mouse
That ruled the house
Chased by Tom, a black cat
Who was a useless prat.

Then lo and behold along came this bunny
Called Bugs, who was very funny.

A park ranger who talks to a bear
That man really should be taken into care
Yogi, what sort of name is that
He's completely off his hat
And just what would you do
If your mate was called Boo Boo.

It was just my luck
To bump into a Daffy Duck.

Well no more jokes
That's all Folks.

A STATE OF MIND

Someone once asked me
Why are you called Yogi
I replied perhaps I'm a mystic
And some names just stick.

GHOST TRAIN

I was travelling by train
Thro' France to Spain
A trip of emotional cost
To a place of love lost.
Landscape so barren then green
Places I've already seen
A journey to exorcise your ghost
And revisit our jovial host
Clickety clack clickety clack
Along seemingly endless track
Mile upon boring mile
Then my eyes caught her smile
And with just a glance
My journey of remembrance turned into romance.

NO STORY

I read this book recently
It was called a dictionary
Word after word
Some I've never heard
But I have to complain
Why does the writer need to explain
All the words in such detail
I couldn't follow the tale.

BLOB

Onto paper I dropped some ink
Its appearance made me think
As across the paper it spread
Is there a message to be read
Tea leaves leave pictures for some to see
What is that blob telling me.

AT FACE VALUE

I was sat in this boozer
Saw this man, a total loser
Picked on a lad small in size
Boy was he in for a surprise
He was left bruised and hurt
The lad was a kick boxing expert

Doesn't matter who you may come upon
It's best never to underestimate anyone.

ICE AGE

Now I'm feeling so cold
Young but oh so old
Cast aside like a used bag
Treated as if I was just a rag.
Walking down an endless avenue
Stupid as I am, I still love you.

AIR MAIL

One evening whilst walking in Berkeley Square
Happy go lucky without a care
An avian left me a message I couldn't ignore
That nightingale will not be singing anymore.

AND THEY'RE OFF

If you want to keep the burglars out
There's no need to scream and shout
Just put a Des O'Connor cd on
And they will soon be gone.

READY MEAL

Strolling by the river for a while
When I bumped into this crocodile
He didn't seem very happy
Actually he was quite snappy
After a chat I thought now he's alright
Until he licked his lips and took a bite.

GENIUS

She wrote a musical score
Of life on the bleak Yorkshire Moor
A story of love gone wrong
Emotions portrayed in song
Wuthering Heights in rhyme
Was the hill she had to climb
Musical convention swept aside in a rush
This is the genius of Kate Bush.

BANK HOLIDAY

Young girls and boys without sins
Just broad cheeky grins
With joy they scream
As they eat their ice cream
On donkeys they ride
Enjoying a day at the seaside
They bring a big smile to my face
And leave me in a happy place.

SWIMMING LESSON

The frog chased by a dog
Jumped into the bog
The dog went charging in
Soon learnt how to swim
Crafty frog hopped onto a log
And safely drifted into the fog.

JUST LAZY

Some people don't know what hands are for
Haven't the brains to open a door
See a button that says 'open here'
Couldn't even open a bottle of beer
Very soon you will find
A machine will have to wipe their behind.

CRASH LANDING

It was just by luck
That I saw this duck
It was funny and nice
To see it trying to land on ice
I thought if it did tricks
It could be in the Aquacktic Olympics.

www.ingramcontent.com/pod-product-compliance
Lightning Source LLC
Chambersburg PA
CBHW072016060426
42446CB00043B/2568